Warman's®
Coca-Cola®

FIELD GUIDE

Allan Petretti

Values and Identification

©2005 Allan Petretti

Published by

kp books

An Imprint of F+W Publications

700 East State Street • Iola, WI 54990-0001
715-445-2214 • 888-457-2873

Our toll-free number to place an order or obtain
a free catalog is (800) 258-0929.

Library of Congress Catalog Number: 2004098434

ISBN: 0-89689-138-0

Designed by Wendy Wendt and Jamie Griffin

Edited by Dan Brownell

Printed in the United States of America

Dedication

To my wonderful wife, Rannie, and my three great children, Dante, Deanna, and Vito, who have shared their husband and father with Coca-Cola for all these years...I love you all.

Contents

Go Refreshed

Introduction

The history of Coca-Cola is one of the most remarkable stories in American business. The creator of the drink, Dr. John Stith Pemberton, began his career as a pharmacist and became successful developing and selling proprietary medicines. Pemberton's desire to create the perfect medicine and drink led him to experimenting with a substance derived from coca leaves that was supposed to aid digestion and extend life.

In 1886, Pemberton also developed a coca and cola drink that according to legend, he tried out at the Venable soda fountain at Jacob's Pharmacy in Atlanta. To produce and promote the drink on a commercial scale, Pemberton and his partner, Ed Holland, started the Pemberton Chemical Company with two other businessmen, one of whom named the drink Coca-Cola. Pemberton received a patent for the drink in June 1887, but sold the majority of his interest in the company within a year. The ownership of the company changed hands a number of times after that, but it was well on its way to becoming one of the largest and most successful companies in the country.

Public fascination with Coca-Cola goes far beyond the fact that it has been America's number one soft drink since its humble beginnings in 1886. The truth is that its success is based on more than great taste and high quality. That kind of longevity and success requires a combination of excellent product, good business practices, loyal employees and the foresight to make advertising a top priority. Coca-Cola's advertising is what this book is all about. Fortunately, items are available at all price levels, so virtually anyone can collect them.

Scope of this Book

This field guide, as well as my full-sized book, *Petretti's Coca-Cola Collectibes Price Guide, 11th Edition*, only deals with original, true "vintage" Coca-Cola advertising and production material, and has a cut-off date set in the early 1970s. New, commemorative, and made-for-the-collector-market items aren't listed, as they comprise an entirely different market. I also don't list vending machines, because many fine books about these machines have been written by authors far more knowledgeable in that area than me.

Because of space considerations, this field guide presents only a fraction of all the resources provided in my full-sized book, *Petretti's Coca-Cola Collectibles Price Guide, 11th Edition*, which contains thousands more listings and photos, and provides much more extensive information and advice about collecting Coca-Cola items. The ad on the last page of this book gives information about ordering copies by telephone or by Internet.

Pricing

The values in this book are not assigned arbitrarily. Years of tracking this memorabilia, supported by a program of consistent and thorough research, provide the basis for evaluating each and every piece shown. Do keep in mind, however, that when all is said and done, it basically comes down to one person's opinion—mine in this case—and the prices listed here are only meant to provide collectors or dealers with an approximate value of a particular item.

Factors Affecting Value

Potential buyers should carefully consider the following questions before purchasing. If a piece is not perfect, what is its condition? Is that condition acceptable? Will it be easy to resell in its present condition? Is it a common or rare piece? How much is the seller asking? And, most importantly, how badly do you want the piece?

Condition

Keep in mind that values shown are based on what I call "average price for average condition." Basing values on some standard such as "mint" condition does a real disservice to all collectors, mainly because most vintage pieces found today are not in mint, or even near-mint, condition. In fact, most pieces are found in excellent or "8" condition, or what I call "average" (see pages 39-43 for Condition Guide). For that reason, prices shown in this book use the "8" condition as the standard. Pieces found in better condition will, of course, command higher prices, while those in lesser condition will be valued lower. This system is designed for flexibility, allowing both buyers and sellers to describe actual condition in an objective manner, whether positive or negative, in order to give each party a better bargaining position.

As more collectors become concerned about their collections, the demand for higher quality pieces continues. The result is that choice pieces in mint or near-mint condition continue to rise sharply, while pieces in average condition increase at a slower pace and, in many cases, items in poor condition do not increase in value at all.

The values shown here are not meant to be absolute. Rather, they are offered to you as a guide to assist you in making informed decisions. Remember, when a transaction is taking place, the buyer and seller ultimately determine the value.

Future Value of Coca-Cola Collectibles

Tracking the Coca-Cola collectibles market is like tracking the stock market. All of us have seen specific areas of the collectibles market rise and fall. Baseball cards, Pez, toys, slot machines, etc. can be red-hot one year but cool off the next. Coca-Cola memorabilia, because of the wide range that is available, will also experience areas that are very hot for a period, followed by a period of little activity. But Coca-Cola memorabilia generally is, and has been, a good solid growth collectible. One must also understand that a slowdown in a particular area of collecting is both normal and expected, especially after a long period of growth. Some consider this a weakening in the market, when in fact it is just the market correcting itself.

The past and present are relatively easy to understand and explain, but what about the future? Will interest in this beautiful memorabilia remain strong? Will items continue to rise in value? Will new collectors continue to enter the market?

I, for one, remain very optimistic. I have watched this market grow from the early 1970s, when all the known collectors could have held a meeting in a phone booth, through the 1980s and 1990s, which saw steady growth and consistent numbers of new collectors entering the market. I have no reason to doubt that this market will continue on its present course because Coca-Cola is a superior product.

Collector Tips

General and Specialized Collecting

People enjoy collecting Coca-Cola memorabilia for many reasons. Surely one of the greatest attractions is the wide range of collectibles available. While most collectors collect anything with the famous Coca-Cola logo, others are specialized collectors.

Because of the expense involved, it may be difficult for one collector to amass a great collection encompassing all areas. But that same collector could have a fantastic collection in one specific area. Many enjoy collecting only Coca-Cola bottles, for example. Others have set a goal to have every tray or calendar the company has produced. But when trying to track down items from the early or pre-1900s, they suddenly realize that it is quite a task.

One of my favorite specialized areas of collecting, and one that even the new collector can get into without spending a fortune, is postcards. Any postcard showing a nice Coca-Cola sign is a good item. Postcards are easy to find, and early ones are very desirable. But whether you collect everything or choose to specialize, you'll always have a good feeling when you add an attractive piece to your collection.

Evaluating Condition

Condition is the most important factor in determining the value of an item. That's why it's so difficult to put a value on an item in a book like this. People often don't consider condition. This is a major error. The price should always reflect the piece's condition.

It would be a mistake to purchase a piece for $50 because it is in the price guide for $50 but the condition is poor. You should point out to the dealer any flaws in the piece and the price should be adjusted accordingly.

I have always been in favor of the "upgrade" system of collecting. This means buying a piece that's available now, but buying a better piece when it becomes available and selling the lesser piece to help pay for the better one. Keep in mind that it's not easy to resell pieces in poor condition, so be sure to consider condition carefully when purchasing.

Detecting Fakes and Reproductions

It's unfortunate but true: fakes and reproductions are a part of collecting. Whether it be Coca-Cola items, Ming vases or teddy bears, reproductions are everywhere. The trick is to keep your mistakes to a minimum, and the best way to do that is plain and simple education. Read everything available and ask questions. Put your mistakes behind you and learn from them. Also, tell other collectors about items that you know are phony.

Finding out if a piece is original or reproduction is important, but questioning the dealer is not always the answer. Don't be fooled by appearance. Many pieces can be instantly aged by unscrupulous dealers who are looking to make a buck from the collector who is anxious to make a major find.

I wish there were a perfect way to know a reproduction from an original, but there isn't. I suggest seeing the original, holding it in your hands and feeling it. In many cases, this is the best and surest method of not getting burnt.

Tall Tales: Discerning Truth from Fiction

People who deal in antiques and collectibles sometimes attempt to enhance a piece with a fictitious or embellished history to add to its mystique. The challenge is to separate fact from fiction, and learning about what you collect is the best way to do this.

The people who make up these stories usually don't have the correct information to back up the fantasy they have created. It's your job as a collector to get as much information as you can and then analyze it to determine the truth. You must have already heard some of the stories: found in a warehouse, bought from an old bottling plant, discovered in the rafters of an old house or in an old woman's trunk that has never been opened, and my personal favorite: acquired fom an old store that has been boarded up since 1920.

Unfortunately, most of these old stories are used to enhance a phony piece rather than an original piece. Rely on common sense rather than the story to make the decision whether to buy or not. Many people have told me "the piece can't be a phony because the dealer told me he bought it from a woman who had it for fifty years." Do your homework, study the trademark logos on pieces used over the years and how they have changed. So, if a piece is presented to you as found in a treasure chest that has been buried since 1905, but the trademark logo is of 1950s vintage, you'll know right away the piece is phony. (See Coca-Cola logos on pages 44 to 48.)

One of my pet peeves is the misuse of words or phrases like "rare," "very rare," "only one known to exist," "never seen before," "the only one I have ever seen," "only one of three known"—the list goes on, but you get the idea. Take these stories and overused phrases with a grain of salt and realize that they are part of dealing in antiques and collectibles.

Cleaning and Restoring

Of all the tips one can give to the collector, this is certainly the most delicate. Can you imagine someone telling you how to clean and polish a tray, then trying it, only to find that you have totally destroyed it? Well, believe me, it's happened to people many times—especially with trays and metal signs.

Other than simple dusting, leave the piece alone unless you know exactly what you're doing. Some collectors have been successful with dirt removal, cleaning and polishing, but many have learned through trial and error. This is another area where education is important.

Touching up trays or signs is also difficult. It should never be done without complete knowledge of what you're doing. Keep in mind that a tray that's been touched up, whether or not it is a good job, does not have the same value as a piece that hasn't been touched up. Many times a touched-up piece is difficult to sell.

As far as paper is concerned, the same rules apply. Don't do anything unless you know what you are doing. I do strongly recommend protecting paper items, especially calendars, in an album or frame. And finally, always choose a frame shop that uses acid-free mat board and is knowledgeable about paper preservation.

Buying Restored Pieces

When buying a piece for resale or for your collection, it's important to know if it has been restored. Ask the seller what has been done, examine the piece carefully, looking for breaks in the paper or uneven color. If the piece is framed, ask if you may take it out to examine it, as framing and matting can hide damage. If the dealer won't let you take it out, be very skeptical. Also be sure when buying a piece that it can be returned if you discover it has been restored after being told it wasn't. From a collector's standpoint, you would like everything in your collection to be in original mint condition; however, this is just not realistic, especially with something as delicate and rare as early paper. You should be aware that a piece of restored advertising, no matter how rare or how well that restoration was done, can't be called mint and will never have the value of a unrestored piece, even if *looks* unrestored.

You must decide if restored pieces are acceptable, and if so, how limited or extensive the restoration can be. There will always be a range of standards for restoration among collectors, and setting standards for your collection is your choice, not mine or any other collector's. However, when setting your standard, keep in mind the potential appreciation and resale value of your pieces.

Collecting Coca-Cola as an Investment

Many collectors of Coca-Cola memorabilia consider themselves only collectors and not investors. This is a mistake. People collect for different reasons—they enjoy the hunt, they are taken by the visual appeal or perhaps they like owning of a piece of the history of The Coca-Cola Company. But regardless of your motivation for collecting, every dime spent on a collection is money that had to be earned, and that makes your collection an investment.

The same rules apply with buying collectibles as with any other investment. Most important is to know the market in which you are dealing, getting as much information about Coca-Cola collectibles as possible. People who invest in the stock market research the market and the company they are seeking to invest in. The same thing that has to be done when buying a piece for a collection. To determine if a piece is a good investment, use the following guidelines.

The first is a very touchy one and I'm sure to get flack over it, but I suppose I'm just a Coca-Cola purist. I really believe that buying newer items is not a good investment. I have been buying and selling Coca-Cola pieces for a long time, and prices for vintage pieces have risen year after year, but not for the reproduction, fantasy and newer collectible items.

Many think the size of a collection is very important. I've heard many boast of having thousands of pieces in their collection, and to accomplish this they will buy anything and everything bearing the Coca-Cola logo. Don't fall into this trap! Many of the recently produced items for the collectibles market that sell for $5 to $10 today may not even be worth what you paid for them 10 to 15 years from now. If you ask anyone who has tried to sell a collection loaded with commemorative and newer items, you'll find that it's not easy. Even when the collection is sold, the collector usually ends up taking a loss.

On the other hand, those who have sold collections of original advertising pieces found it easy and have made large profits. I would rather have a smaller collection of quality older items than a larger collection of newer items. When I say "older," I don't necessarily mean items from the '30s rather than the '50s, but rather items that weren't purposely produced for today's collectible market. Because these "made for the collector's market" items are made in huge quantities, they won't appreciate in value and don't make good investments.

However, "made for the collector's market" items do serve at least one purpose. They introduce new collectors to the hobby, and a percentage of them trickle down to collecting vintage items. This continual influx is what keeps me so positive about the future. And there's nothing wrong with buying "made for the collector's market" items, as long as you're buying them for enjoyment and not for an investment.

Financing Your Collection

Over the past 10 or 12 years, I've seen the prices of Coca-Cola collectibles rise constantly, and unless you have just hit the lottery or are independently wealthy, it can be very difficult to amass a nice collection. But there are ways to finance your collection as long as you are willing to spend some money.

I have heard many people say that they have passed up a worthwhile piece because they already have it in their collection. This is a mistake. If you are at a show and see an item that you feel is priced right, you should buy it, even if you have it or if it is in a different area than your collection. You can sell it for a profit or use it for trade.

Another good way to make money is to create a list of items for sale, such as upgrade items or duplicates. Advertise in the club newsletter. Let other collectors know that you have a list of items for sale. (Remember to keep close track of what you pay for items and what you sell them for.) Soon you will have a little nest egg for use when you want to purchase a special piece for your collection.

Finding Coca-Cola Collectibles

When people see my collection, one of the first things they ask is: "Where do you find all this stuff?" It isn't easy, and it takes a lot of time and hard work to build a collection. Even if you have a fortune to spend, it isn't always that easy to find quality pieces. For this reason alone, Coca-Cola collecting is a challenge, and adding a beautiful piece to a collection becomes exciting.

It's important to let collectors know who and where you are and what your interest is. One must also keep abreast of what is happening in the field of antiques and collectibles. Subscribing to publications such as *Antique Trader* and other newspapers and magazines devoted to collectors is one of the most important links to people who have pieces for sale, and an excellent way to let people know your wants. These publications also list antique shows and auctions in and out of your area. I have a good friend who travels often, and he never leaves home without checking the *Antique Trader* to see what shows will be taking place in the area where he will be traveling.

Check auction listings in antique and other publications as well. Many good Coke pieces have been hidden away in a general auction with no competition from other collectors. Subscribe to auctions and try to get on mailing lists of auction houses, even if they don't specialize in Coke or advertising items. Coca-Cola pieces turn up in most auctions eventually.

Stay alert, don't assume that an all-furniture auction, for example, has no Coke items in it. Ask questions to be sure. Large antique shows all over the country sell anything and everything in antiques and collectibles, while many other shows specialize in advertising, coin-op, paper items, toys, etc. All of these are good sources of Coca-Cola memorabilia. Know when and where they are, and then be there.

Some collectors find placing inexpensive "want ads" in local papers to be a great source of items right in their own backyard. Local antique shops are another important stop. Go to the ones in your area on a regular basis, leave your card, let them know your interests, and ask them to give you a call if anything turns up.

Many towns have areas heavy with antique shops or malls that specialize in antiques and collectibles. Year-round, weekend antique shows are also very popular. Find out where they are and visit them, perhaps as part of a day trip or a long weekend with the family. Buying nice stuff and building a good collection takes work. Coca-Cola pieces don't come to you—you have to go out and find them.

Getting Involved in the Collector Community

Becoming involved in the collecting community is important. Know who the collectors are and where their interests lie. Most Coca-Cola pieces change hands between existing collectors, either through the upgrade system or through collectors selling off individual pieces or sections of their collections. Read books and, of course, ask questions.

Find out what pieces were recently found and for how much they sold. Know the market and remember that an informed and knowledgeable collector is a collector who will eventually end up with a good collection. I can't tell you how many times I have heard comments like, "I've been collecting for years, and thought I was the only one!" and "I had no idea this stuff was worth this much!" The more you know about the subject, the better off you'll be.

Try to meet and get to know collectors with interests similar to yours. Asking them questions, and possibly seeing their collections, is very helpful in making informed decisions regarding your own collection. Don't be afraid to let people know what you collect.

I find that networking with other collectors is the best way to stay abreast of this ever-changing market. Call or e-mail fellow collectors to find out what you may have missed. I have also found that networking helps the market eliminate "phony" collectibles.

Buying Through Internet Auctions

Large numbers of Coca-Cola items are now sold on Internet auction sites such as eBay. While these sites provide a convenient and popular way to buy and sell, they can involve more risk than buying or selling in person. Sellers typically include photos as well as descriptions, but photos don't show every flaw, and descriptions can be inaccurate.

One safeguard is the feedback system, in which buyers and sellers rate each other on their satisfaction. If you choose to use an Internet auction site, make sure you check the potential buyer's or seller's feedback. If you have questions, be sure to e-mail or call the person and get satisfactory answers before bidding. Also be sure you know the payment, shipping, insuring and return policies.

Buying at Live Auctions

Live auctions are great sources of Coca-Cola collectibles because they display excellent artwork. Many pieces were saved and turn up at house sales and auctions. Be sure to subscribe to mail auctions and antiques publications, and make sure you're aware of sales in and out of your area. Many auction houses will accept absentee bids, so don't be afraid to ask and to use your phone. It can save you a lot of wasted time. I can't tell you how many miles I have traveled to auctions because a creative auctioneer listed in his advertisement "very rare Coke tray" only to find a 1950 tray that looked like it had been run over by a truck.

On the other hand, though, I took a six-hour trip to an auction that listed a Coke sign that turned out to be one of the most important pieces I have ever purchased. Those pieces are the ones that make it all worthwhile.

Get to know your local auctioneers. If you trust them, tell them your interests. Believe me, the next time they have a Coke piece, they'll let you know. If a piece is listed in the advertisement, make a call and ask for a description and the condition. Go to the sale preview, but don't run up to the piece and reveal your enthusiasm.

Another tip, as difficult as it may be, is to set a limit on what you will spend. Many great Coke pieces have sold at auctions far below their value because they just didn't have the right audience. But many pieces have sold far above their value because the right group of people was in the room.

Keeping Records

It's extremely important to keep an accurate, up-to-date record of every piece in your collection. Remember, you're investing as well as collecting. Every piece that you spend money on or trade for is an investment that should be recorded. List every piece with its date of purchase or sale, amount paid, condition and any other pertinent details.

If you have been collecting for some time and haven't done this, do so as quickly as possible. Listing each and every item is a big job, but believe me, it should be done. This is also important if you decide to sell your collection or perhaps leave it to a spouse or children. A current record is the backbone of every collection.

Insuring

Not being an insurance agent or knowing your collection, I can't tell you how to insure it. But I can give you some hints. You shouldn't assume that your collection is covered on your homeowner's policy. Don't assume anything when it comes to insurance. Call your agent, invite him to inspect your collection and get his advice. If you're not happy with what your agent tells you, call another and then another if necessary, until you find a policy that you feel comfortable with.

Collections can be insured in several ways; for example, you could increase your homeowner's policy by adding a rider that covers the collection. Or you could possibly take out a "fine arts" policy to cover some of the more expensive items.

You may be required to keep a photographic record of your collection for your insurance company. This, by the way, is something that I recommend whether it is required or not. Try to set a minimum value for the items that are to be photographed.

Displaying

Proper framing is essential to protect your investment. Make sure the person doing the framing uses the proper paper conservation methods and is aware of the value and importance of the piece. It's extremely important that the framer doesn't do anything to the piece that you haven't discussed, like gluing, trimming or removing anything from it, such as a metal strip or calendar page. Also, make sure the framer is insured to cover your piece while it is in his possession, and put that on your receipt with the value. Point out the importance of using acid-free mats and backing as well as using a spacer such as a mat so the printed piece doesn't touch the glass. If the edges of the piece are sharp with no tears or edgewear, don't cover the edge with a mat, so if you should ever decide to sell it, the potential buyer can see that nothing is hidden.

Be sure pieces aren't exposed to high

humidity or direct sunlight. Hooded frame lights work well for small quality pieces, but track lighting is best for large areas. The ability to move individual lights to eliminate glare is a big advantage, but eliminating all glare from a room with many framed pieces is just not possible. Using nonglare glass in frames can help, but I personally don't use it because it dulls the colors.

Serving trays and tin signs require a lot more attention and should be checked periodically when displayed. Some people do frame certain trays and tin signs, and that's fine, but make sure a sealed, framed piece can breathe, meaning it isn't airtight. Avoid areas with high humidity, and polish with a mild car wax once every year or two to prevent pitting. The best place to display tin is in an area with a fairly constant temperature.

Showcases are especially good for displaying pocket mirrors, watch fobs, knives and celluloid pieces. If you don't have room for a large showcase, small flat ones are available.

Storing

Paper signs, calendars and cardboard pieces that aren't displayed require proper care for storage. Purchase sheets of foamcore and a roll of thin, clear acetate from an art supply store. Measure the piece and allow an extra quarter inch all around. Cut the foamcore to this size. Don't attach the piece to the foamcore with tape or glue; simply place the piece face-up on the foamcore, then flip the foamcore and sign face-down on a rolled-out section of acetate. Cut the acetate, leaving plenty of excess. Pull the acetate tightly across the back of the foamcore, and tape it. Cut the ends, and again pull tightly and tape. Foamcore and acetate aren't cheap, but the cost is well worth the protection.

To move or store trays, always put them in clear plastic bags. This is the best way to protect them from scratching.

Flat paper items like blotters, coupons, magazine ads, letterheads and other paper collectibles are best kept in plastic sleeves that can be filed in a three-ring binder for easy access. Books, paper items and other collectibles can be stored in corrugated file boxes. Pack the items, label the outside of the boxes and store them off the ground in a dry area.

Condition Guide

The condition of any Coca-Cola collectible is the most important factor in determining its value. Collectors use two types of grading systems. Nowadays, the "Poor" to "Mint" system seems to be used less than the "1" to "10" method. On the following pages are both systems with representative photos of a 1934 tray. Please keep in mind when evaluating an item that it is not in anyone's interest to overgrade it.

10

9.5

9

8.5

8

7.5

7

6.5

6

5.5

Mint

New condition, unused, flawless, no visible marks or scratches. There is no middle ground in this category; it's either perfect or it's not. You can't say "It's Mint but it has a scratch."

Mint = Perfect.

Near Mint

Very minor or slight marks, chips, or scratches, a minor tear (on paper). Nothing serious that would detract from the color or beauty of the piece. This is the category most often misused.

Excellent +

Visible minor scratches, perhaps minor chips, minor tears or peeling of paper items. Excellent is the category most pieces fall into and the one that prices in this book are based on.

Excellent

Just a few more minor chips than normal, scratches, minor marks, but still not serious, a repairable tear on paper items. Still a very good looking piece and very collectible.

Very Good

This is the extreme low end of Excellent condition. Still collectible, but a few more problems; perhaps a white spot on a tray, slight pitting, edge chips and rubs, a few tears or a small piece out of the edge of paper items.

Good

Scratches, minor flaking, possibly minor dent and rust or pitting, serious tears, or portion missing on paper items. An OK item. This is the point when it becomes questionable whether the piece is collectible or not.

Fair

More than minor pitting and flaking, dents, trimmed or torn paper, fading or bad color. Collectible only if it's a rare piece; a good filler item.

Poor

In worn state, with rust, dents, or pitting. A paper item that has been torn and repaired, possibly restored; generally not very collectible.

Poor

Extensive pitting and rust areas, extensive fading and wear, dents and bends, restoration work that has been done poorly. This would be an item that would not be collectible or have much value at all.

Worthless

An item that has no redeemable qualities, something that you would not display regardless of rarity; something you didn't have to pay for.

The Coca-Cola
Script Trademark

The story surrounding the creation of the Coca-Cola script trademark is an interesting one, and since it has never been disputed, the legend lives on. Pemberton's associate Frank Robinson named the product for two of its ingredients, changing the "K" in "Kola" to a "C." It was also Robinson, as the story goes, who penned the famous script lettering that is now so familar, although this early script version was probably not used until 1887.

The script lettering, or logo, has changed and has seen many variations over the years. Following are many of those variations. Study them, because knowing these logos and when they were used can be very helpful in determining age, as well as detecting counterfeit pieces. Keep in mind that many of the companies producing advertising for Coca-Cola, and especially local Coca-Cola bottlers, took liberties with the logo, in some cases altering or misusing logos, or even using an outdated logo, especially in the earlier years.

1880s-1892
Early script variation with diamonds

1890-1891
Unusual typestyle used on a number of calendars

1887-1890
Early script with line extending from first "O"
"Trade Mark" in tail; also no trademark in tail.

1893-1901

Crude script with "Trade-Mark" in tail,
under tail or no trademark with
"Trade Mark Registered" in tail 1901-1903

1898-1902

Custom script with "Trade-Mark" in tail;
note open "O's", and unusual tails on "C's"

1903

Misused script "Trade-Mark Registered"
in tail; used on some 1903 calendars.

1903-1931
Traditional script "Trade-Mark Registered" in tail

1930-1941
Traditional script "Trade-Mark
Reg. U.S. Pat. Off." in tail

1941-1962
Traditional script "Reg. U.S. Pat. Off." under script

1950-Present

Traditional script "Trade Mark ®" under script

1958-1963

"Arciform" logo also called
"Fishtail" logo by collectors

1970-Present

"Dynamic Ribbon" also called "Wave"
logo; actually introduced in late 1969

Calendars

It isn't a coincidence that calendars appear first in this book. They have been, since my first day as a collector of Coca-Cola memorabilia, my main interest. I would have considered trading any tray or sign I owned for a particular calendar I needed.

Many people don't realize the importance of the calendar as a marketing tool in the days before radio or television. Of course, newspaper and magazine ads and signs brought the product before the public eye, but the calendar was much more than that. It was a useful product that was given away to consumers with the hope that they would hang them in their homes to remind them that Coca-Cola was "delicious and

refreshing." It obviously worked, and worked well. The Coca-Cola Company realized this, producing at least one type of calendar every year beginning in 1891. In some cases, several calendars were produced in a year.

During my early years of collecting, only one group of price guides was available for Coca-Cola collectibles, and the discrepancies between the calendars shown in these guides and the calendars I was purchasing were obvious. It soon became clear that many of the calendar pads shown were switched or altered in some way. Those price guides, unfortunately, are still available, showing the misdated and altered calendars. With this book, I hope to clear up those discrepancies.

Prior to 1914, calendar sizes weren't very consistent. The size of a complete calendar (including pad) made between 1914 and 1919 is approximately 13" x 32". From 1920 to 1922, they measured 12" x 32". All of these calendars were equipped with a metal strip and hanger at the top.

From 1923 to 1940, the size was approximately 12" x 24", again with metal strip and hanger. In 1926, however, the calendar changed drastically, measuring 10-1/2" x 18-5/8" and printed on medium-weight cardstock. It also had a hole drilled at the top for hanging (replacing the standard metal strip). This was also the first year that the calendar had a cover sheet over the pad. It simply said, "1926 Compliments of The Coca-Cola Co., Atlanta, GA." Cover sheets over the pad weren't standard until after 1930.

Another interesting aspect of Coca-Cola calendars is the glass and bottle variations. Because of the obvious difference between fountain and bottle sales, two calendars were issued in certain years, with one model holding a glass and the other a bottle. In some cases, one type of calendar may be rarer than the other, depending on how many have turned up over the years.

The following is a list of years in which calendars were printed with both glass and bottle versions: 1904, 1914, 1915, 1916, 1917, 1919 (knitting girl), 1920, 1923 and 1927. The 1923 bottle version is very unusual in that the bottle is embossed "8 oz." rather than the standard "6 1/2 oz.," which was the size of the bottle used at that time.

The 1927 calendar also has a slightly different variation. On one calendar, a large bottle is inset with a border around it on the lower left-hand side, and another has no bottle at all.

The 1928 distributor calendar also has a glass variation. In 1918, and from 1921 to 1930 (with the exception of 1923 and 1927), calendars show both glass and bottle. From 1931 on, they show bottles only.

As any collector who actively seeks Coca-Cola calendars knows, they aren't easy to find. Any calendar before 1914 is considered rare, and any before 1910 is very rare. Despite the rarity of these early calendars, the value drops drastically if they are found without a pad or a sheet attached, or if they are trimmed from their original size.

After 1940, there was a major change in Coca-Cola calendars. From 1941 through the 1960s, they were made as multiple-page calendars, usually of six pages plus a cover sheet, with two months on each page.

The condition of the calendar, as with

any Coca-Cola collectible, is most important in determining value. The prices you see on calendars in this book reflect examples in clean, presentable condition. Examples in poor condition or without a pad will certainly be worth less, and mint untouched examples could certainly be worth more.

Keep the following things in mind when purchasing a calendar. First, be sure that it has not been trimmed from its original size. (The measurement information provided earlier should be helpful.)

The pad or sheet attached is also important. Make sure it is the correct year for the calendar. If it is not a full pad, take note as to how many sheets are attached. One sheet attached (other than the last sheet) is acceptable as long as you realize that you are buying an altered calendar. If a calendar is trimmed or has a partial pad or no pad at all, or had been mounted to poster board, it can't be called mint.

Whether you are a die-hard calendar collector like me, or you just happen to have a few in your collection, I hope you'll agree that calendars are certainly the most beautiful of all Coca-Cola collectibles.

Condition plays a crucial role in value! Items in this book are priced based on a condition rating of "excellent" or "8" (see pages 40-41 of Condition Guide). Items in mint condition, or "10," could be worth more than the listed price, while items in fair or poor condition could be worth much less.

The items shown in this chapter are just a cross-section of the vast amount of memorabilia that Coca-Cola has produced. This sampling, however, should give you a good idea of what is available and their general values.

1891, 6-1/2" x 9".....................................$18,000
Photo courtesy of Gordon Breslow

1891, 6-1/2" x 9". **$18,000**

1896, 6-1/2" x 9". **$25,000**
Photo courtesy of Gordon Breslow

1897, cut down as shown........................$4,500
Complete with pad $25,000

1898, 7-1/4" x 12-3/4"
.... $20,000

1899, 7-3/8" x 13"
.... $15,000

1900, 7-1/4" x 12-3/4" $20,000
Photo courtesy of The Coca-Cola Co.

1901, 7-1/4" x 12-3/4"
.... **$20,000**
Photo courtesy of Gordon Breslow

1901, 7-5/8" x 11"
.... **$13,000**

1901, 7-3/8" x 13".............................$8,500

1902, 7-1/2" x 14-1/2"
.... $10,000

1903, 7-3/4" x 15"
.... $7,000

There are two versions
of this calendar.

1904, 7-3/4 x 15" $6,500

1905, 7-3/4" x 15-1/4"
.... $7,000

1906, 7" x 14-1/4"
.... $8,000

1907, 7" x 14" $8,500

1908, 7" x 14" $7,000

1909, 11" x 20-1/2"
.... $10,000

1910, 8-3/4" x 17-1/2" $7,500

1910, "Happy Days," 15" x 26" $13,000

1911, 10-1/2" x 17-3/4" $6,500

1912, 9-3/4" x 19-3/4", small version
....$6,000

1913, 13-1/2" x 22-1/2"
.... $5,000

1913, 16" x 28", bottler's
calendar $10,000

1914...................... $2,500
With bottle (not
shown) $6,500

1915...................... $6,500
With bottle (not
shown) $9,000

1916, with bottle
.... $3,500
With glass (not shown)
.... $3,500

1917, with bottle .. $4,500

1918...................... $9,500

1919, with glass..............................$6,500

1919, with bottle .. $6,500

1920, with glass.... $4,000

1922...................... $3,600

1923, with bottle .. **$1,200**

1924..................... **$2,000**

1925...$1,500

1926...................... $1,900

1927, glass only.... $1,800
With bottle inset (not shown) $1,600

1928..$2,000

1929...................... $2,000

1930...................... $2,000

CARRY ME BACK TO OLD VIRGINNY

1934.......................................$1,000

1935..........................$850

1936...................... $1,100

1937...........................$850

1938...........................$850

1940..$850

1941..........................$550

1942..........................$450

1944.......................................$450

1945..........................$450

1946..........................$850

1948.................................$400

1949.........................$375

1950.........................$375

1951.......................................$225

1952.........................$200

1953.........................$225

1954.......................................$185

1955..................$125

1956..................$100

1957 ....$125

1958 ....$85

1959 .... $100

1960..$75

1961............................$75

1962............................$75

1963..$75

1964.............................$75

1965.............................$75

1966... $75

1967 ....$75

1968 ....$75

1969.............................$75

1970.............................$75

Distributor Calendars

1916, 8" x 15", Miss Pearl White $5,000

This calendar was a magazine insert piece.

1918, 5" x 9", June Caprice
...................................$500

1919, 6-1/4" x 10-1/2",
Marion Davies....... $5,000

1927, 7" x 13" $2,000

1928, 8" x 14" $850

This calendar was produced
in other variations.

Bottlers' Calendars

1915, Western Coca-Cola Bottlers..$6,500

1928, Romney, W.V.
.... $3,500

1953, 16" x 33-1/2",
Kentucky Derby $1,800
Photo courtesy of Gordon Breslow

1946, 6-1/2" x 11-1/2",
Art, Boy Scouts, Rockwell
.....................................$400

1949, 8" x 14-1/2", Art,
Boy Scouts, Rockwell
.....................................$400

1958, 11" x 23", Art, Boy Scouts, Rockwell $450

1964, 7-1/4" x 10-1/4", Cub Scouts $200

Home Calendars

1954...$20

1955.......................................$20

1956...................$20

1957 .... $18

1958.................$18

1959.................$16

1961 .... $12

1963...................$12

1964...................$12

1965 .... $12

1966 .... $12

1967 .... $12

1968 .... $10

Serving Trays

When I first started collecting Coca-Cola memorabilia, serving trays were the main point of interest. It seemed that everyone's collection was judged by which trays they had and which trays they needed. Early price guides reflect this fact. While other items were shown, the most important were the serving trays. Even The Coca-Cola Company produced a book in 1970 called the *Catalog of Metal Service Trays and Art Plates Since 1898,* which seems to be the first book on the subject, and in fact, on Coca-Cola collecting in general.

Because of the importance of trays, I find collectors have placed more emphasis on their condition than the condition of other pieces. The typical tray collector considers every little scratch and dent on a tray. That's why it is so difficult for a book like this to place values on trays, and I must stress, once again, that the prices you see here are just guides. In other words, they're average prices for clean, presentable trays (excellent or better condition). If a tray is rough, the price will be lower, and with more common trays, much lower. If the tray is in mint condition, the price certainly can be higher. And just because a tray sells for a fortune at an auction, that doesn't mean that price is the true market value. It's very possible that two people just got carried away with the moment.

While it's quite possible that earlier trays do exist, the so-called 1897 "Victorian Girl" tray has always been thought of as the first and certainly the most important and most difficult to find of the trays. The earliest known trays, from 1897 through 1901, were 9-1/4" round. A 9-1/4" round tray was also used in 1903 in addition to a larger oval tray.

In 1905, The Coca-Cola Company produced a smaller oval tray. This seemed to have continued until 1909 with a series of medium and larger oval trays. Tip or change trays varied from 4" to 6" circular types until 1907, when they became standard 4-1/4" x 6" ovals until 1920, after which they were no longer produced.

Beginning in 1910, a rectangular tray was made, measuring 10-1/2" x 13-1/4". It became standard and was used into the early 1960s. Between

1910 and 1919, rectangular trays were produced only in 1910, 1913 and 1914. In 1916, a completely different tray was produced measuring 8-1/2" x 19". Subsequently, no trays were made until after World War I. Then, in 1920, production resumed on a regular basis, with at least one tray each year until 1942, and then no more until after World War II.

Most of these rectangular trays have appeared in sufficient numbers to keep collectors happy. However, most collectors strive for a mint or at least a near-mint example, neither of which is easy to find.

After World War II and into the 1950s and 1960s, the production of trays was, at best, spotty and irregular. TV trays, plastic trays and commemorative trays replaced the popular and beautiful Coca-Cola girls of the 1920s and 1930s.

Displaying trays has always been a minor problem with collectors. Everything from magnets, plate hangers, and glue and string have been used, some successfully, while others not. I personally think the best way to display a tray is to lean it on a narrow shelf with an edge.

But however you display your trays, it's essential to protect them. The most important thing is to avoid humidity. Don't store or display trays in a damp area such as game room or bar in a basement unless you use a dehumidifier, or they will gradually become pitted.

The other big problem with trays is dust. It always seems to accumulate on the bottom rim of the tray. If this dust is allowed to build up, it will be difficult to clean and could certainly detract from the tray. If trays are not cleaned and dusted properly, you will create a series of light scratches. With all of these warnings, I am trying to stress the fact that you must take care of your trays if you want to retain their value.

Whether you simply collect particular trays that strike your fancy, or you strive to own every example known, the serving tray is the classic Coca-Cola collectible.

Condition plays a crucial role in value! Items in this book are priced based on a condition rating of "excellent" or "8" (see pages 40-41 of Condition Guide). Items in mint condition, or "10," could be worth more than the listed price, while items in fair or poor condition could be worth much less.

The items shown in this chapter are just a cross-section of the vast amount of memorabilia that Coca-Cola has produced. This sampling, however, should give you a good idea of what is available and their general values.

1897, 9-1/4"
....................$30,000

1899, 9-1/4"
....................$20,000

1901, 9-1/2" $8,000

1903, 9-1/4"..$7,000

1903, 15" x 18-1/2"
.....................$10,000

1903, 9-3/4", bottle tray $12,000

1905, 10-1/2" x 13", with glass $5,000

1906, 10-1/2" x 13-1/4" $5,000

1907, 10-1/2" x
13-1/4", medium
oval................$4,000

1907, 13-1/2" x
16-1/2", large oval
........................$8,500

c.1908, 12-1/4",
"Topless Tray"
.........................$7,500

1909, 10-1/2" x
13-1/4", medium
oval................$3,000

1909, 13-1/2" x 16-1/2", large oval.................................. $4,500

1913, 12-1/4" x
15-1/2"............. $850

1914, 12-1/2" x
15-1/4"............. $650

1910.............$2,000

1913.............$1,000

1914..$900

1921..............$1,200

1922................$950

1923.................$550

1924, red (maroon)
rim.................$1,300

1924, brown rim
.... $850

1925 .... $575

1926..............$1,000

1928, fountain sales
..........................$950

1929, fountain sales $600

1928, bottle sales
.........................$1,000

1929, bottle sales
.........................$750

1930, fountain sales
............................$550

1930, bottle sales
............................$600

1931.. $1,000

1933.................$850

1934.............$1,000

1935.................$500

1936.................$500

1937.................$375

1938.................$300

1939..$375

1941.................$400

1942.................$400

1950-52, screened
background $85

1950-52, solid
background $250

1953-60.............$65

1957................$300

1958................... $40

1961................... $30
At least three versions were made.

Tip/Change Trays

1901, 6" $3,500

1901 variation,
5-5/8"............$4,500

1903, 6" $2,000

1903, 4" $3,500

1903, 5-1/2", bottle
tray $10,000

1907, 4-1/2" x 6" $1,000

1909, 4-1/2" x 6"
.........................$750

1910, 4-1/2" x 6"
.........................$800

1913, 4-1/2" x 6"
.... $700

1914, 4-1/2" x 6"
.... $350

1916, 4-1/2" x 6"...................................$285

Vienna Cut Plates

Framed $2,500
Without frame
..........................$850

Framed $550
Without frame
..........................$275

Framed $675
Without frame
.... $350

Framed $1,000
Without frame
.... $650

Framed $675
Without frame $375

Framed $675
Without frame
..........................$350

Framed $1,000
Without Frame
..........................$700

Reverse side of art plate imprinted in center. These plates can also be found with other or no advertising on back. They have much less value, and have nothing to do with Coca-Cola.

Plates/Change Receivers

c.1907, 7", change receiver, glass, The Empire Ornamental Glass Co., N.Y. $2,500

1931, 7-1/4", sandwich plate, E.M. Knowles China Co. $400

1969, 14", frozen Coca-Cola change receiver, plastic $150

Signs

Trolley Signs

Trolley cars, also called street cars, were first introduced in New York City in 1831. Originally, the trolleys were horse-drawn carriages that operated on tracks in the street. At the end of the 19th century, most major American cities built street railways, but it wasn't until electric street cars were introduced that street railways came into widespread use. The first electric trolley was installed in Richmond, Va., in 1887.

Unfortunately, because of the ever-growing popularity of the automobile, the street railway system began to decline and eventually die. But, in their time and because of their low cost and convenience, the trolleys were a popular form of public transportation and, therefore, an excellent place for companies such as Lucky Strike, Nabisco, and of course, The Coca-Cola Company, to target their advertising.

This advertising came in the form of cardboard signs, which collectors have dubbed "street car signs" or "trolley car signs." They are unmistakable because all are a standard size of 11" x 20-1/2", printed on a lightweight, flexible cardboard. The size of these signs was very important, because they were inserted into standard sized metal brackets, and the selling and changing of the signs was done by advertising agencies, many of which specialized in trolley advertising.

Have a Drink of *Coca-Cola* DELICIOUSLY REFRESHING

Young boys, hired by the ad agencies, usually changed the signs. One boy would stab the old sign with a sharp, pointed stick and lift it out with one swift motion. Another boy would follow and pick up the old signs. And yet another boy would insert new signs into the brackets. With the demise of the trolley as a major form of transportation, similar signs were used on buses and subways.

For collectors, trolley car signs have always been one of the most desirable and sought after of all Coca-Cola signs. Unfortunately, early ones are very rare. Because of the type of material they were made of and their exposure to the heat and the cold, trolley car signs are usually found in rough condition. Also, many of the signs are discolored because of smoke from smoking passengers.

Large Signs

Certainly the most difficult pieces to evaluate in a book such as this are large signs. Smaller versions are usually more appealing because most collectors lack sufficient display place for the larger ones. "Displayability" is the highest priority for most collectors, who believe they can use space better by displaying a number of smaller signs than one large one. Consequently, the value of large signs will vary much more than their smaller counterparts. Personally, I'm not interested in 5-foot, 6-foot or 8-foot signs at any price. I don't collect them, nor do I have a good market for selling them.

On the other hand, dealers and collectors who supply restaurants and taverns with these signs for decoration have a good market and will pay well for them. So unless you can find the right buyer, selling a larger sign is sometimes a real problem. I have received many letters and calls over the years from frustrated collectors who can't understand why they can't find a buyer for their 6- or 8-foot porcelain sign.

Therefore, before buying such a sign, ask yourself a few questions: Do I have the space to display this piece? Do I have the patience to find the right buyer? Do I also realize this sign will not appreciate in value like the smaller signs? Also keep in mind that the values shown are based on collector desirability for such signs.

Kay Displays

Beginning in 1934, Kay Displays, Inc. of New York City, produced signs and advertising displays for The Coca-Cola Company. Although the stamping on the back of many of these signs state "Designed & Manufactured by Kay Displays, Inc.," the company only designed the displays and didn't actually manufacture them. The owner and president of the company had a good working relationship with American Seating Co., of Grand Rapids, Mich. American Seating was an ideal partner for Kay Displays because it was able to produce the quantity and quality required by The Coca-Cola Company.

Before World War II, Kay and American Seating used various materials such as embossed lithographed tin, stamped metal, ornate cutout tin, wood, cardboard and composition

material. But with the approach of the war and constant demand for metal, display advertising was limited to material that would not interfere with the arms buildup.

Many of the Kay Designs produced from Dec. 7, 1941, to the end of the war reflected the patriotism and unity that swept the country. A pair of spread wings with a raised hand and bottle emblazoned many of the signs of this period and are among the most desirable of all Kay creations.

With the war over and the metal once again available, Kay's specialty signs took a back seat to the quickly produced, inexpensive and long-lasting tin signs that The Coca-Cola Company was again using by the millions. Consequently, Kay Display went out of business in 1951. But the Kay Display will live on forever in the hearts and collections of the individuals who appreciate its contribution to Coca-Cola advertising.

Condition plays a crucial role in value! Items in this book are priced based on a condition rating of "excellent" or "8" (see pages 40-41 of Condition Guide). Items in mint condition, or "10," could be worth more than the listed price, while items in fair or poor condition could be worth much less.

The items shown in this chapter are just a cross-section of the vast amount of memorabilia that Coca-Cola has produced. This sampling, however, should give you a good idea of what is available and their general values.

c.1896, 30" x 40", Cameo paper sign, printed by J. Ottman Litho, Co., N.Y.
.... **$25,000**

Pre-1900 paper signs are very rare.

1901, 14-1/2" x 19-1/4", "Girl with Yellow Roses"
.... **$15,000**

Beware of repros of this piece. Original has "copyrighted 1898 Wolf & Co., Phila." on lower right corner. One repro has a signature on left corner of table and cross (+) mark or marks on chest or table.

1902, 14-3/4" x 19-1/2", bottle sales **$17,000**
Photo courtesy of Christian Daniel

1902, 14-3/4" x 19-1/2", fountain sales..... **$16,000**

1903, 14-3/4" x 19-1/2", Hilda Clark......... **$17,000**

1904, 14-1/2" x 19-1/2", Lillian Nordica, metal strip, rare............ **$15,000**

1908, 14" x 22", "Good to the Last Drop," metal strip top and bottom, very rare **$17,000**

1913, 18" x 24", "Which? Coca-Cola or Goldelle Ginger Ale," rare............. **$10,000**
Photo courtesy of Dave Baker

1912, 16" x 24", printed by Ketterlinus Co., Philadelphia, Pa. ... $5,000

c. 1912, 16" x 22", printed by Ketterlinus Co., Philadelphia, Pa... $6,500

1920s, 13" x 22", heavy paper $1,800

1920s, 29-1/2" x 43", printed by The Forbes Lithograph Mfg. Co., Boston, Mass., very rare $8,500

Late 1940s, 36" x 52", Amsterdam.............$350

Trolley Signs

1910, featuring "The Coca-Cola Girl" by
Hamilton King and printed by Wolf & Co.,
Philadelphia, Pa. $7,500

1912.. $7,500

1914... $7,500

c. 1912, "Whenever You See An Arrow"
....$2,000

c.1912.. $5,000

c.1918...$5,000

c. 1913, 11" x 20-3/4"..............................$5,000

1914, 11" x 20-3/4"..................................$5,000

1923, "The Four Seasons"..........................$3,000

c. 1927..$3,500

Cardboard Signs

1896, 6-1/2" x 10-1/2", hanging sign,
cardboard...................................... $20,000
Photo courtesy of Scott Rosenman

1905, 26" x 46", Lilian
Nordica, rare **$15,000**
Photo courtesy of
the Brinker Collection

1909, 28-1/2" x 45",
cardboard sign, rare
.... **$16,000**

1921, 18" x 30", paper sign........................ **$2,500**

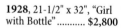

1928, 21-1/2" x 32", "Girl with Bottle" **$2,800**

1920s, 10" x 14", "Hot Dog," rare....$2,800

Late 1920s, 10" x 10", "Designed and Printed in Canada" (lower left)
.... $1,700

1929, 19" x 31" $2,000

1938, 21" x 44" $500

1935, 13" x 21", two-sided hanging sign
....$750

1935, 13" x 21", two-sided hanging sign
....$800

1936, 29" x 50", 5oth Anniversary...........$3,000

1938, 34" x 50", "Girl with Roses," inside store display $3,000

1936, 27" x 56", rare $3,600

1936, 12-1/2" x 33", litho in Canada..................$750

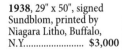

1938, 29" x 50", signed Sundblom, printed by Niagara Litho, Buffalo, N.Y........................ $3,000

1940s, 29" x 50".................................. $950

1946, 29" x 50" $700

1948, 29" x 50" $1,000

1956, 29" x 50", "Travel Girl".......................... $550

1942, 29" x 50", "Snowman," Niagara Litho $750

1942, 29" x 50", "Two Girls at Car,"
Edwards & Deutsch Litho.............. $1,000

1944, 16" x 27", with gold wood frame.......... **$1,200**

1943, 16" x 27", with original frame **$1,000**

1942, 16" x 27", "Umbrella Girl," Snyder & Black $650

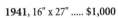

1941, 16" x 27" $1,000

1940, 16 x 27".....................................$600

1946, 16" x 27" $700

1942, 16" x 27", "Girl in Rain," Snyder & Black
.... $800

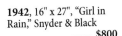

1941, 16" x 27", "Girl Skater," Niagara Litho Co. $650

1942, 16" x 27"," Young Couple," McCandlish Litho..........................$600

1947, 16" x 27" $800

1945, 16" x 27" $600

1948, 16" x 27" $600

1948, 16" x 27" $500

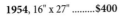

1954, 16" x 27" $400

1957, 16" x 27", "Snowman," with gold
wood frame.. $600

1949, 16" x 27" $400

1948, 16" x 27" $450

1952, 16" x 27" $400

1952, 16" x 27" $300

1950, 16" x 27" $400

1956, 16" x 27" $300

1956, 16" x 27" $400

1939, 27" x 56" $2,400

1941, 20" x 36", with original gold wood frame............ $1,500

1943, 20" x 36" with rare version of gold wood frame.. **$1,200**

1944, 20" x 36", with gold wood frame **$1,200**

1942, 27" x 56", McCandlish, Litho. $750

1942, 27" x 56", "Picnic Grill," Snyder & Black $750

1940, 27" x 56", with original gold wood frame............ $1,800

1940s, 20" x 36", with gold wood frame........................... $950

1944, with gold wood frame... $1,000

1948, 20" x 36", with gold wood frame $850

1945, 20" x 36", with original gold wood frame................**$850**

1945, 20" x 36", with original gold wood frame................**$750**

1948, 23-1/2" x 41"...$650

1949, 20" x 36" $800

1938, 20" x 36" $850

1948, 20" x 36" $450

1953, 20" x 36", with original gold wood frame............ $1,200

1942, 20" x 36", with original gold wood frame................ $800

1957, 20" x 36", "Me Too," with aluminum frame............ $750

1950, 20" x 36", with gold wood frame $850

1950s, 20" x 36" $600

1952, 20" x 36" $500

1956, 20" x 36" $400

1950s, 20" x 36" $300

1950s, 27" x 56", with aluminum frame...........................$450

1960s, 20" x 36", with original aluminum frame..............$225

1953, Sweetwater Clifton
.....................................$700

1953, Alice Coachman
.....................................$700

1953, Sugar Ray Robinson
.....................................$750

1953, Ted Rhodes.....$450

1953, Jesse Owens
.... $1,000

1953, Buddy Young
.... $600

1949...$600

1949.........................$600

1949.........................$600

1951..........................$650

1949...........................$600

1950s, 12" x 15", in aluminum frame................................$700

1950s, 12" x 15", in
aluminum frame.......$700

1950s, 12" x 15", in
aluminum frame.......$500

1950s, 12" x 15", in aluminum frame.................................$500

1959-1960, 14" x 18-1/2", Ricky Nelson $700

1956, 15" x 16", two-sided $325

General Cutouts

c.1890s, 5-1/2" x 8-1/2", display piece, easel
back, Wolf & Co., Phil., Pa.........................$7,000

c.1890s, 6-1/2" x 7", display piece, easel back............... $8,000

c.1909, 5' x 6', foldout window display, very rare when found complete... $16,000

1910, 28-1/2" x 39-1/2", "Man in the Grass" (with glass), printed by American Lithography $7,500

This cutout also exists in a bottle version.

c.1912, 30" x 46", "Soda Fountain," window display, cardboard cutout **$10,000**

c.1912, 29" x 38", "All the World" **$8,500**
Photo courtesy of Gordon Jakway

1913, 30" x 35", "Couple at the Beach" (with glasses).. **$8,000**

This cutout also exists in a bottle version.

c.1911, 29" x 36", "Sundial" $8,500

c. 1918, 18" x 27", printed by Ketterlinus,
Philadelphia, Pa. $7,500

c.1917, paper die-cut, part of a set of window trim $2,500

1924, 24" x 40" $8,000

1916, 28" x 42" $6,000

1930, 18" x 42" $2,200

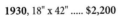

1926, 28" x 42" $4,500

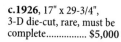

c.1926, 17" x 29-3/4",
3-D die-cut, rare, must be
complete................ $5,000

c.1903, 4-1/2" x 10-1/2", cardboard sign, easel back, embossed, die-cut, Kaufman & Strauss Co., N.Y. **$16,000**
Photo courtesy of Chuck Campbell

c.1903, 4-1/2" x 10-1/2", cardboard sign, easel back, embossed, die-cut **$16,000**

1922, 32" x 40", "Girl on Aqua Plane," fold-out window display
.... $8,500

1925, 15" x 20", cameo, easel back display.................... $2,000

1925, "People at Soda Fountain," fold-out
window display, 23" x 33"..........................$1,600

1920s, "Dahlia," window display fold-out, art
from a painting by Carle Blenner............... $850

1937, 8-1/2" x 14",
Canada $850

1939, 12" x 16", (French)
Canada $350

1932, Dorothy Mackaill, easel back, Niagara Litho Co. $1,500

1932, Loretta Young, easel back, Niagara Litho Co. $1,500

1922, 19" x 19-1/2".. $6,000

1926, 18" x 32", "Umbrella Girl," with bottle................ $3,000

1933, 25-1/2" x 35-1/2", window display......................... $5,500

1931, 19" x 27", Norman Rockwell Art, shown incomplete
(dog missing) $2,500

1935, 18" x 36", Norman Rockwell Art, printed by Snyder & Black $3,800

1927, 13" x 30", "Circus Girl"..........................$750

This piece is actually part of the circus window display.

1944, 62-1/2", "Woman Shopper" display
.... $1,000

1940s, 23" x 31", easel back $700

1944, 15" x 19", cardboard cutout display (Niagara Litho), 3-D hanging or stand-up (another Sprite Boy version exists), rare
.... **$2,700**

1950s, 10" x 12", Phil Rizzuto $1,000

1956, 18" x 19" $425

1947, display sign.....$135

1950, 7" x 7", string
hanger $35

1950s, 36" x 60", "Cowboy," mechanical point of purchase display, hands and eyes move ...$1,800

c.1963, 15" x 30", easel back display $375

Festoon Cutouts

1914, "North South East West" (shown without end pieces),
rare $18,000
Complete, very rare $23,000

c.1918, "Umbrella Girls" $6,500

1920s, "Lantern" festoon, rare...................................... $7,500

1932, "Verbena" $3,000

1960, "Birthstones" **$1,000**

1950s, "Know Your State Tree" **$575**

Santa Cutouts

1941, 32" x 42", Santa window display $1,500

1946, 6" x 12" $385

1954, 10-1/2" x 19"...$325

1953, 9" x 18" $375

1962, 32" x 47" $425

1950s, 36", easel back
.....................................$275

1949, 15", easel back
.....................................$375

1950s, 18" x 27", 3-D...$200

1948, 7-1/2" x 13-1/2"
..................................$475

1955, 19", easel back
..................................$100

Bottle Displays

1929, 7" x 9-3/4", "Winter Girl," bottle topper, rare..$3,200

1923, "Bottle Displays," cardboard cutouts, American Litho., N.Y. .... $1,000 each
Complete set of four $5,000

1920s, 10" x 14", "Boy with Weiner," cardboard cutout $3,500

1938, cardboard cutout, (French) Canada $1,000

1940, 21" x 40", carton display, 3-D cutout,
actual six-pack slides under hand $1,100

1936, six-pack display....$775

"6 for 25¢" $550

1950s, bottle topper, plastic **$1,000**

1950s, cardboard fold-up bottle display **$45**

1950s, two bottle display, metal (France) ..$600

Banners

c.1908, 16-1/2" x 46", unusual paper sign with bottler's name, rare $4,000

1950s, Eddie Fisher and Kit Carson TV shows, 34" x 68" $200

1950s, 36" x 66", coin coolers $300

1951, 11" x 22" $125

1944, 8" x 25", Sprite Boy $350

1950, 11" x 24" $250

1950s, 11" x 22" $85

1954, 11" x 22" $125

1950s, 13" x 41" $85

1952, 11" x 22" $100

Metal Signs

1899, 20" x 28", Hilda Clark, embossed tin, rare
.... $20,000

1920s, 6" x 12", hanging sign, celluloid........................ **$1,800**
Photo Courtesy of Larry Dikeman

1922, 4" x 8", tin, embossed.. **$750**

1920s, 4-1/2" x 12", tin over cardboard.................. $750

1931, 4-1/2" x 12-1/2", tin, embossed $650

1930s, cooler sign, white porcelain with black trim.........$950

1930s, bottle shaped aluminum door handle $450

1930s, porcelain push plates, Canada .... $400 each

1960s, 4" x 6", push-pull plates .... $185 each

c.1908, 12" x 36", Spanish.. $2,000

1930s, 5-3/4" x 17-3/4", embossed tin............................... $375

1931, 20" x 27", embossed tin (in bottles variation) $1,000

1929, 20" x 28", "Gas Today," embossed tin $3,000

1934, 19" x 28" $800

1940s, 20" x 28", also made in masonite $450

1941, 20" x 28" $650

1950s $1,600

1960s, 18" x 54" $400

1950s, 20" x 28"..$275

1963, 20" x 28" $275

1950s, 16" x 50"..$700

1964, 11" x 28"..$275

Flange and Tin Cutouts

1936, 16", 50th Anniversary, embossed tin.................. $2,500

1950s, 11" x 12", six-pack sign...........................$950

1950s, 11" x 12", six-pack sign...........................$950

1950s, 16", tin $385

1939, flange sign $650

c. 1948-50, flange sign $800

1960s, flange sign $300

Porcelain Signs

1933, 10" x 30", porcelain, Tenn. Enamel Co. **$1,200**

c. 1939, 14" x 27", masonite $900
Porcelain version.. $1,500

c. 1950s, 28" x 28", porcelain, made in both one-sided and two-sided versions **$1,500**

1949, 12" x 29", porcelain $525

c. 1950s, 12" x 18", porcelain $525

c. **1950**, 16" x 16", die-cut porcelain flange, Canada..... $2,500

1952, 12" x 29", porcelain, Canada $550

c. 1950, 12" x 28", porcelain $650

1950s, 16" x 22", porcelain, England $1,000

Button and Disc Signs

1950s, 16", button sign with arrow, white, rare $2,000

1952, 10" x 36", wood and masonite with 12" disc $1,000

1950s, 16", German porcelain $500

1950s, 16" x 40", with bottle $1,000

1950s, button calendar sign $450

1950s, spinner for top of vending machine $1,200

Glass Signs

1932, 12" x 20", reverse glass sign, red version, with chrome frame and chain, rare, Brunhoff Mfg. $5,000

Note: There is also a black version of this sign.

1920s-Mid 1930s,
11-1/4" dia., reverse
glass mirror sign,
..........................$575

1950s, 10" dia.,
reverse glass sign,
beveled edge,
Germany $950

1950, reverse glass sign on wood base $750

1949, 18" x 22", reverse glass hanging sign, two-part, Price Bros. $2,000

Celluloid and Plastic Signs

c.1950s, 9", celluloid hanging sign $300

c.1940s, 9", celluloid hanging sign $350

c.1950s, 9", celluloid
hanging sign, rare
........................$1,500

1950s, 10" x 12",
pressed plastic easel
back..................$200

Light Up Signs

1920s, 18", leaded glass shade, "Chain Edge" $6,000

"Property of The Coca-Cola Company - To Be Returned on Demand" appears twice on the top metal band.

Late 1930s, 12" x 14", reverse glass, "The Brunhoff Mfg. Co."
.... $5,000

1939, 15" x 20", neon hanging sign, rare
....$5,500

Late 1940s, 18" x 42", neon hanging sign.....................$1,700

1950s, 17" x 17", plastic front, with cardboard insert.......$650

1950s, 9" x 20", pause (motion) light-up counter sign
.... $1,800

1950s, 8" x 18", glass print, metal frame............................$500

c.1960, 18" x 32", plastic light-up, rotating
display, shown complete............................$1,000

Clock Signs

c. 1910, 4-1/2" x 4-1/2", gold stamped leather $3,000

1930s, 5" x 9-1/4", cash-register-top sign/Sessions clock, Cincinnati Advertising Products, Cincinnati, Ohio, rare $4,500

1939/40, 17-1/2, "Spinner" neon clock.........................$5,000

c. 1939, 23", Spinner clock, neon, Electric Clock Co., Columbus, Ohio $3,600

1939-42, reverse glass, metal frame $1,200

1950s, metal.... $650

1950s, light-up glass
front $650

1951, 17-1/2",
maroon.............. $250

1951, 17-1/2", silver
.... $275

1960s, plastic... $175

1960s, glass front
.............................$400

1960s, plastic...$200

Thermometer Signs

1930s, 17", tin $500

1939, 6-1/2" x 16", tin
.....................................$400

1941, 7" x 16", gold
.....................................$450

Can be found with 1940 date.

1944, 7" x 17", masonite
....$450

c. 1948, 9" $300

1950s, 12", glass front $300

1957, 12", glass front $300

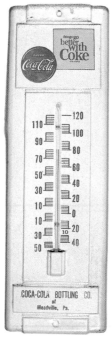

1960s, 4-1/2" x 14", tin
.....................................$200

1960s, plastic............$100

Miscellaneous Signs

1930s, 12-1/2", composition, Kay Displays $1,800

1930s, 7', tin and wood festoon, Kay Displays $4,500

Late 1930s, 12" x 30", wood hanging sign, Kay Displays
.... $3,000

c.1941, 9-1/2", stamped composition............................ $2,000

c. 1939, arrow sign, wood and aluminum $900

1930s, 9" x 11", wood with metal trim, Kay Displays $700

Late 1930s, 11" x 39", wood cutout hanging sign, Kay Displays
....$950

1930s-40s, 10-1/2" x 14", hanging sign, wood, Kay Displays
.... $1,000

1930s, 12" x 32" (each), wood with metal trim, Kay Displays
.... **$1,600 each**

1940s, two-part wood and tin hanging sign set............ $1,200
Each.. $450

1940s, menu board, wood with metal trim, shown with bottom piece missing.. **$475 as shown**

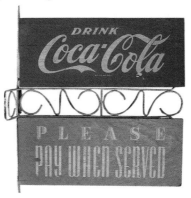

1950s-60s, two-sided, wood sign with metal trim **$500**

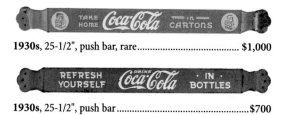

1930s, 25-1/2", push bar, rare.. **$1,000**

1930s, 25-1/2", push bar...$700

1960s, 24", produced in many sizes $400

Bottles

Bottles have long been a favorite among collectors of Coca-Cola memorabilia. A fascinating variety of styles, shapes and colors were used through the years, although most collections seem to focus on the various cities where Coca-Cola bottling franchises have existed.

The earliest bottles known to contain Coca-Cola were of the Hutchinson stoppered variety. The words Coca-Cola appear in either block print or script lettering on the bottles, and embossing usually designates the city where the bottle was originally filled. Hutchinson bottles were used only briefly and by fewer than a dozen bottling works just after the turn of the century. Relatively few have survived.

In the early 1900s, crown-top, straight-sided bottles replaced the heavier, cruder Hutchinson bottles. Millions of crown-top bottles were used by the ever-increasing number of Coca-Cola franchises between 1902 and 1915. Few records were kept, however, and individualism was rampant. A given Coca-Cola bottling works might use bottles of several different styles and colors at various times. Some bottles had fancy designs such as rings, shields or arrows embossed onto the glass; still others had slug plates identifying the then proprietor of the Coca-Cola franchise. All straight-sided bottles displayed a paper label identifying the product they contained and bore the Coca-Cola trademark embossed in script lettering as well.

The early crown-top bottles were hand blown in molds, with their necks and lips finished by special hand-held tools. Such techniques often left rough seams, irregular patterns of thick and thin glass, numerous bubbles and imperfections in the glass itself, and sometimes crooked shapes. Machine-made crown-top bottles with fewer deficiencies and evenly formed seams began to replace the hand-tooled bottles after 1910. The variety of glass colors used ranged from clear and aqua to differing shades of blue, green and amber. Even the amount of liquid a bottle contained varied considerably

since 6, 6-1/2, 7, and up to quart-size 24- and 26-ounce
bottles existed. The script writing Coca-Cola trademark
sometimes appeared at the base of the bottle, sometimes in
the center and sometimes on the shoulder. While this lack
of uniformity creates interesting collections of straight-sided
Coca-Cola bottles, the inevitable confusion generated by such
diversity eventually led to the adoption of the now famous
"hobbleskirt" or "Mae West" shaped bottle as the standard
glass container for Coca-Cola shortly after 1915.

The first patent for hobbleskirt bottles was issued on
Nov. 16, 1915, to the Chapman Root Glass company of
Terre Haute, Ind. The patent was renewed on Dec. 25, 1923.
Such "Thanksgiving" or "Christmas" Coke bottles, as they
are sometimes called, have become quite popular among
collectors because the base plate of most of these bottles bear
the name of the city where they were first filled.

Well over 2,000 cities are known to have been home to
Coca-Cola bottlers as the bottling network expanded. The
classic shape has received several patent renewals since 1923,
and hundreds of millions of hobbleskirt bottles were put into
service over the years.

Many bottles can be found on which the words Coca-Cola
or "property of Coca-Cola" appear in block letter print only.
Although some of these bottles are of the older, hand-blown

variety, most date from the 1920s or later. Collectors generally agree that these block letter bottles probably didn't contain Coca-Cola, but rather the various fruit-flavored drinks that were handled by individual bottling franchises. Often these bottles had paper labels identifying the kind of soda water they contained. Larger, quart-size bottles were also used this way.

These "block letter" bottles come in a variety of colors and shapes, and make for an interesting collection of their own. A surprising number have fancy embossings, such as people or animals. But very few, if any, were ever used for Coca-Cola, and the "flavor bottles" generally do not have the value of bottles that actually contained Coca-Cola.

Two other types of bottles deserve mention. Syrup bottles did indeed contain genuine Coca-Cola syrup obtained from the parent company in Atlanta and were used at sit-down soda fountains to hand-mix one's 5-cent drink with carbonated water. Many of these tall, clear glass bottles have the words Coca-Cola in acid-etched lettering or printed on paper labels sometimes sealed under glass. The trademark appears on such bottles in block lettering or in script.

Certain Coca-Cola franchises also bottled and sold seltzer water to local outlets such as bars, restaurants and soda fountains. This was done in a variety of beautifully colored or clear glass siphon bottles with acid-etched lettering or applied color labeling. The words Coca-Cola are found on these bottles in both block letter or script writing styles, although such bottles were used for seltzer water only and never to dispense Coca-Cola.

The relative value placed on Coca-Cola bottles is largely determined by the age of the bottle (Hutchinson, straight-sided or hobbleskirt), its scarcity (small town versus franchise, for example), and the color of the glass and condition of the bottle (free from chips, cracks, cloudiness and considerable wear). An original metal crown or paper label enhances the value of a bottle appreciably.

Condition plays a crucial role in value! Items in this book are priced based on a condition rating of "excellent" or "8" (see pages 40-41 of Condition Guide). Items in mint condition, or "10," could be worth more than the listed price, while items in fair or poor condition could be worth much less.

The items shown in this chapter are just a cross-section of the vast amount of memorabilia that Coca-Cola has produced. This sampling, however, should give you a good idea of what is available and their general values.

Hutchinson Bottles

Script, Jasper, Ala. $3,000

Script, "Property of Coca-Cola" $3,500

Script, Birmingham, Ala.
.... $2,500

No mention of Coca-Cola, Biedenharn Candy Co. $300

Amber Bottles

Knoxville, Tenn..........$65

Clear/Light Green Bottles

Muskogee, Okla. $165

Okmulgee, Okla., rare
.....................................$275

Altus, Okla. $125

Miscellaneous Bottles

1916-1924, embossed, "Bottle Pat'd Nov. 16, 1915" ....$6 to $15

1924-1937, embossed, "Bottle Pat'd Dec. 1923" (Christmas Coke) ....$3 to $8

1937-1948, embossed "Bottle Pat'd 105529," changed to "In U.S. Patent Office" in 1951 ....$1 to $3

1950s, ACL and embossed, "Contents 6 1/2 Fluid Ozs." ....$1 to $2

1960s, ACL, "Coke" on reverse side ......$.50 to $1

Diamond Design Bottles

1960s, 10 oz., diamond $5

1960s, 10 oz., diamond, paper label $550

1960s, diamond, foil label prototype............... $1,000

1960s, diamond, foil label, rare prototype $1,200

1960s, 10 oz., plain diamond, Canada........$35

1960s, ACL, diamond $250

1960s, green glass, multi-diamond, paper label $235

1960s, multi-diamond, paper label $125

1960s, ACL, multi-diamond prototype ..$150

1960s, ACL, multi-diamond prototype ...$150

Front   Back

1960s, ACL, 10 oz., "turn-top" cap $150

1960s, ACL, New Zealand
.....................................$275

1960s, 16 oz., foil label,
screw-top $150

1960s, ACL, 12 oz. large mouth prototype, rare $750

1960s, multi-diamond, screw top, quart $55

1960s, 28 oz., multi-diamond, twist top $65

1960s, ACL, 1 pt. 10 oz., prototype $800

1960s, ACL, 1 pt. 10 oz., prototype....................$800

1960s, ACL, multi-diamond, 1 pt. 10 oz., prototype....................$750

Seltzer/Syrup Bottles

Bradford, Pa............$275   **Susanville**, Calif. $165

1930s, glass syrup jug with paper label and original box
....$450

Cans

1955, first production can, test market from New Bedford, Mass., for export to U.S. troops in the Far East $750

1959, test market can
.....................................$425

1960, first domestic can
.....................................$400

1960, Canada............$175   1960s, Canada..........$500

1961, first bottle diamond $200

1963, second bottle diamond....................$175

1963, third bottle
diamond....................$150

1963, 7 oz. bottle
diamond prototype, rare
.... $1,500

1966, first multi-diamond $65

1960s, second multi-diamond......................$35

1960s, third multi-diamond, all-aluminum......................$75

Bottle Carriers

1924, six-pack carrier,
cardboard.................$375

1930s, six-pack carrier,
cardboard.................$650

Mid-teens to 1930s, vendor's carrier with straw holder, tin
....$750

1930s, six-pack carrier, cardboard $250

c.1938, six-pack carrier, cardboard $185

c.1938, six-pack carrier, cardboard $125

1940s, six-pack carrier, wood, masonite...........$225

1950s, six-pack carrier, aluminum.....................................$200

1950s, six-pack carrier, cardboard $25

1930s, 12 bottle carrier, wood $500

1940s, 12 bottle carrier, wood, rare.....................................$400

1950s, 12 bottle carrier, aluminum $185

Coolers and Ice Chests

1940s, table top ice chest, cooler 17" x 22" rare, small size $2,500

1950s, cooler, France $350

Late 1930s, 12" x 14" x 25", Westinghouse "Half Junior," two versions $1,300

1950s, picnic cooler, vinyl $225

Back

1964-65, World's Fair cooler box, vinyl
.........................$125

Front

Toys and Games

For the first 30 years or so of The Coca-Cola Company's existence, the product was aimed at adults. For example, the company used slogans such as "Relieves Fatigue," "The Ideal Beverage for Discriminating People" and "For Shoppers and Businessmen." It wasn't until the late 1920s and early 1930s that it considered youngsters an important market.

But when the company began catering to children, it did an admirable job. By far the most popular items in this section are the toy cars and trucks. But not all items in this section were produced with children in mind. Playing cards, for example, have always been an important "giveaway" for adults.

Condition plays a crucial role in value! Items in this book are priced based on a condition rating of "excellent" or "8" (see pages 40-41 of Condition Guide). Items in mint condition, or "10," could be worth more than the listed price, while items in fair or poor condition could be worth much less.

The items shown in this chapter are just a cross-section of the vast amount of memorabilia that Coca-Cola has produced. This sampling, however, should give you a good idea of what is available and their general values.

General Toys and Games

1930s, Ideal "Wonder Doll" in original box with insert brochure, Coca-Cola on bottom of doll's shoes. **$4,000**

This doll is rare; very rare with original box.

1950s, 12", Buddy Lee doll, plastic............ **$1,200**

1978, Japanese R2-D2 Coca-Cola radio, in original box, made by Fuji Electric, toy made by Takara, rare **$1,800**

1980s, Cobot in original box $200

1930s, child's baseball glove, "Drink Coca-Cola in Bottles", rare $700

Close-up of baseball glove strap.

1930-31, "Coca-Cola Flyer" three-wheel scooter, 36" long
.... $2,500

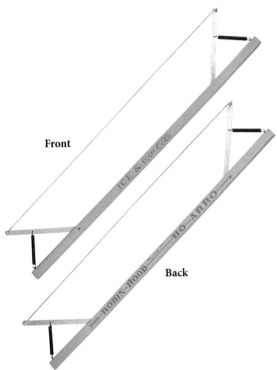

Front

Back

1930-31, Robin Hood BO-ARRO toy bow and arrow $375

Tick-Tac-Toe $225

1940s-50s, bingo set..$75

1940s, bingo card
.... $40

1938, "Steps to Health" Game, Canada $150

1940s, Dominos $65

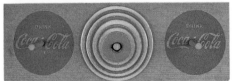

1949, Tower of Hannoi Game $250

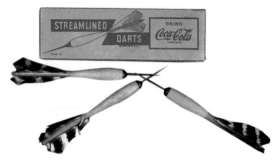

1940s-50s, darts (darts not marked with logo)..................$55

"15" puzzle, wood $225

English.. $400
French, Canadian $325

c.1959 puzzle, London with original box
....$100

c.1979, puzzle, resealable can..$25

Whistles

DIRECTIONS
Fold together and blow. A
tone can be played, etc. Patent
or Rooster instated, etc.
Hold between lips or teeth
when blowing. Used Aft.
April 20, '09, & Feb 7, '10.
E. G. Forsher & Co., Mfrs.
538 S. Clark St. Chicago, Ill.

"MAKE
A
NOISE"

If
Somebody
Tries
To Serve You
Something
"Just the Same"

ACCEPT
NO
IMITATIONS

DRINK
Coca-Cola
IN BOTTLES

THE MOST
REFRESHING
DRINK

IN
THE WORLD

CALL FOR IT BY
NAME
Coca-Cola

c.1916-1920, 5-3/4", cardboard whistle, shown open and closed $750

Miniatures, Radios and Music Boxes

1929, Glascock salesman sample cooler........................ $7,000
1929, mint in original carrying case $16,000

1950s, 7" x 12" x 9-1/2", cooler radio $750

This radio is not difficult to find; it must be working and in excellent condition with original knobs to justify this price.

1950s, 7" x 12" x 9-1/2", cooler radio, Mexico...........$1,000

1950s, cooler music box, different versions $3,000

1950, crystal radio set...$350
Set with original instructions....................................$400

1950, miniature cooler music box (working)....................$225

1950s, plastic vending machine bank $250

1960s, vending machine bank, plastic $125
Bank in box $200

1930s, miniature six pack............................$225

1950s, ceramic case $325

Toy Trucks

c.1932, No. 171 Metalcraft truck, with rubber wheels
.... $1,200

c.1934, Metalcraft, long front, rubber wheels, rare $3,600

1949-50, Goso tractor trailer, wind-up, very rare $2,500

1950s, 5-1/2", GMC truck $1,200

1948, Buddy-L, wood, rare $5,000

Early 1940s, Smith Miller, wood and metal, with wood blocks
.... $2,200

c.1949, Goso, rare $3,500

1950s, Marx, plastic $900

1950s, Marx, plastic.................................. $900

1950s, Marx, plastic.............................. $1,000

1950s, Marx, Sprite Boy......................... $1,100

1950s, Marx $1,800

1950s-60s, battery operated, yellow and white $550

Early 1950s, 7", Marx truck...$600

c.1954, Marx $700

1950s-60s, battery operated, red and white $650

1960s, Buddy-L $475

1948-1950, Italian, wood, tin, and Bakelite, very rare
.... $4,000

1950s, Marx No. 21 (Canadian version), very rare **$1,500**

1959, Buddy-L, orange.. $800

Playing Cards

1909..............$6,000

1928..............$1,200

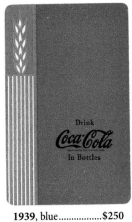 

1939, blue.................$250   **1936**..........................$600

1938...........................$400   1938.......................$500

1943..........................$125   1943..........................$125

1943..........................$125   1943.........................$125

1943..........................$500   1943..........................$500

1956...........................$125   1956...........................$125

1958..........................$145

1958..........................$100

1959...........................$100   1963...........................$100

1963 .... $85   1980s $20

Paper Items

Paper items include smaller advertising pieces like bookmarks, stamp holders, notebooks, postcards, fans, menus and coupons. They are typically practical items that could be used around the home rather than the display items that simply were only for decoration and viewing. The Coca-Cola advertising executives were wise to offer these handy products, as they provided potential customers with constant exposure to their product, as people would read and reread the slogans as they went about their daily lives.

Condition plays a crucial role in value! Items in this book are priced based on a condition rating of "excellent" or "8" (see pages 40-41 of Condition Guide). Items in mint condition, or "10," could be worth more than the listed price, while items in fair or poor condition could be worth much less.

The items shown in this chapter are just a cross-section of the vast amount of memorabilia that Coca-Cola has produced. This sampling, however, should give you a good idea of what is available and their general values.

Bookmarks

1898, 2" x 2-1/4", bookmark, celluloid
.... $700

1900, 2" x 2-1/4", bookmark, celluloid
.... $700

c.1906, 1-1/2" x 3-1/8", "Owl" bookmark, celluloid.. $800

1904, 2" x 6", Lillian Nordica bookmark... $325

1905, 2-1/4" x 5-/4", Lillian Nordica bookmark $700

c.1910, bookmark, celluloid, Mobile, Ala. $800

c.1910, bookmark, celluloid, Mobile, Ala. $800

Stamp Holders, Notebooks and Postcards

1900, 1-1/2" x 2-1/2", stamp holder with calendar, celluloid..$700

1902, 1-1/2" x 2-1/2", postage stamp holder, celluloid $650

1902, 2-1/2" x 5", note pad, celluloid $750

1903, 2-1/2" x 5", Hilda Clark note pad, celluloid $600

1910, "The Coca-Cola Girl" post card, Hamilton King Art $850

1911, "Motor Girl" post card $850

Fans, Menus and Coupons

c.1894, fan showing both sides, rare............................ $4,000

1900, fan, showing both sides $325

1902, 4-1/8" x 6-1/8", menu $900

1904, 4-1/8" x 6-1/2", menu $850

1890s, trade card showing both sides, Wine Coca Co., Atlanta, Ga. $1,200

1901, 1-5/8" x 3-3/8", Hilda Clark "Free Drink" coupon ..$900

1905, 3-3/4" x 7", "Lillian Nordica" ad card with coupon, (front and back shown) $900

Rare when found complete. Coupon must be attached to warrant this price.

1905, 6-1/2" x 9-3/4", "Lillian Nordica" magazine ad with coupon. $325

Beware of smaller size reproduction.

Trade Cards

c.1892, 3-1/2" x 5-1/2", trade card $2,000

1901, 2-1/4" x 3-7/8", trade card, rare $1,700

c.1907, folding trade card, shown open and closed $1,000

c.1910, 6" x 7", sales folder, open, showing both sides $600

Miscellaneous Paper

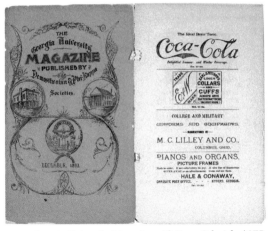

1892, Georgia University Magazine with Coca-Cola Ad...$375

1927, booklet describing "Six-Keys" Contest $25

1930s, cigar bands (glass & bottle) .... **$185 each**

The following is a complete set of 1936 Olympic Games
Schedules, showing front and back of each. Individual
folders are rare, and the complete set is very rare.

Each...$300
Complete set $1,500

Each..$300
Complete set $1,500

Each...$300
Complete set $1,500

Each $300
Complete set $1,500

1941-42, 8-1/2" x 17", paper folder recommending Coke for servicemen...**$100**

1954, mini college pennant, order form with three pennants
....$85

1952, Giants baseball, Wes Westrum $125

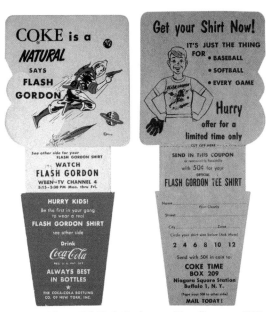

1953, 3-1/8" x 7-1/8", Flash Gordon tee shirt offer $200

1964-65, 11" x 16-1/2" N.Y. World's Fair Coca-Cola Pavilion
Folder $25

Miscellaneous

The Coca-Cola Company has always been a leader in advertising. Even early on, it showed a creativity that would put some modern companies to shame, even though modern firms have access to sophisticated resources like national marketing surveys, computer-generated statistical models, and high-tech television commercials with digitally enhanced graphics.

While the early Coca Cola company didn't have the wonderful resources we have today, it did make the most of what it had available at the time. Coca-Cola put its logo on

almost everything imaginable. And, of course, licensing its name for use on other companies' products was mutually beneficial. The widespread presence of the Coca-Cola logo helped sell the drink, and in turn, the logo gave prestige and visibility to the products of lesser known companies.

Items in this section include figures, pocket mirrors, silverware, pocket knives, ink pens, letter openers, tools, jewelry, smoking paraphernalia and convention badges.

Condition plays a crucial role in value! Items in this book are priced based on a condition rating of "excellent" or "8" (see pages 40-41 of Condition Guide). Items in mint condition, or "10," could be worth more than the listed price, while items in fair or poor condition could be worth much less.

The items shown in this chapter are just a cross-section of the vast amount of memorabilia that Coca-Cola has produced. This sampling, however, should give you a good idea of what is available and their general values.

3-D Objects

1930s, 6-1/2" tall, "Salesman of the
Month" statue....................................... $800

1950s, Sprite Boy napkin holder $1,300

1930s, pretzel dish, aluminum $250

c.1930s, Frozen Coca-Cola stuffed doll........$85

Pocket Mirrors

1906, The Whitehead
& Hoag Co., Newark,
N.J., Duplicate Mirrors
5¢ Postage, Coca-Cola
Company, Atlanta, Ga.
...................................$650

1907, From the painting,
copyright 1906, by Wolf &
Co., Phila., Bastian Bros.
Co., Roch., N.Y., Duplicate
Mirrors 5¢ Postage, Coca-
Cola Company, Atlanta,
Ga. $650

1908, Bastian Bros. Co., Rochester, N.Y., Duplicate Mirrors 5¢ Postage, Coca-Cola Company, Atlanta, Ga. $1,100

1909, J.B. Carroll, Chicago, Duplicate Mirrors 5¢ Postage, Coca-Cola Company, Atlanta, Ga. $600

1910, J.B. Carroll, Chicago, Duplicate Mirrors 5¢ Postage, Coca-Cola Company, Atlanta, Ga. $375

1911, The Whitehead & Hoag Co., Newark, N.J., Duplicate Mirrors 5¢ Postage, Coca-Cola Company, Atlanta, Ga. $325

1914, The Whitehead &
Hoag Co., Newark, N.J.
....................................$650

1916, The Whitehead &
Hoag Co., Newark, N.J.
....................................$425

1920, Bastian Bros. Co., Rochester, N.Y. $850

1931, Spanish (So. American Market), The American Art Works, Inc. Coshocton, Ohio, rare $3,500

Small Items

c.1910, watch fob, celluloid $1,200

c.1912, 1-1/2" dia., watch fob, celluloid,
showing both sides $3,200

1920s, "Safe Driving Award" pin, enameled, rare $500

1940s, 1-1/4" five year no accident pin $100

c.1905-1915, nickel silver, four blade knife $600

c.1913-1915, brass door knob $600

1947, 1-1/4" x 2-1/2", belt buckle, sterling silver $500

c.1920, 4", hat pin, chromed $300

c.1920-1930, saber or sword opener, two different examples
.... **$300 each**

c.1920, blotter pad, celluloid cover, Woodward, Okla. **$400**

1920s, silverware .... **$185 each**

1940s, 10" dia., sundial, bronze...................................... $3,000

1950s, mechanical pencil (bottle clip) $30

1940s-50s, letter opener, chrome.. $85

c.1929, 12-1/2" long, axe "For Sports Men", mint in original box.. **$2,500**

1930s, crowbar, Greenwood Coca-Cola Bottling Co.........**$450**

1968 Olympics (Mexico), 4-1/4", pin tray, sterling silver sombrero, two gold applied plaques, Coca-Cola logo and Olympics logo $750

1950s, tie clip, enameled $100

1963, bookends, bottle shaped, bronze $275

Smoking Items

c.1908, match safe, celluloid, made by Whitehead and Hoag, showing both sides, rare $4,000

1910, "The Coca-Cola Girl" matchbook, showing both sides
.... $1,600

1912, matchbook showing both sides $1,000

1960s, mini can lighter
....$65

1930s, "pullmatch"
ashtray................... $2,500

1936, 50th Anniversary ashtray, porcelain, personally signed at the 1936 convention, rare $850

1950s, ceramic ashtray..............$165

1958, foil coasters

Each...$7
Set of three $35

1958, foil coasters

Each..$7
Set of three $35

1958, foil coasters

Each...$7
Set of three $35

Convention Badges

1916, convention medal, porcelain inlay $1,000

c.1930, convention badge..$125

1939, convention badge $135

c.1943, convention badge..$85

Index